WILLIAM OF WYKEHAM

IMPRESSION OF GREAT SEAL OF
WINCHESTER COLLEGE

IMPRESSION OF GREAT SEAL OF
NEW COLLEGE

WYKEHAM'S EFFIGY ON HIS TOMB IN WINCHESTER CATHEDRAL   FRONTISPIECE

WILLIAM OF WYKEHAM

PATRON OF THE ARTS

By

Sir William Hayter

WARDEN OF NEW COLLEGE, OXFORD

1970

CHATTO & WINDUS

LONDON

Published by
Chatto and Windus Ltd
40 William IV Street
London W.C.2

*

Clarke, Irwin & Co. Ltd
Toronto

SBN 7011 1582 3

Printed in Great Britain by
R. and R. Clark Ltd
Edinburgh

CONTENTS

COLOUR PLATES

MONOCHROME PLATES

PLATES CONTINUED

Personal Note

For a great part of my life I have lived on the charity of a fourteenth-century bishop, as a scholar of Winchester College from 1919 to 1925, as a scholar of New College from 1925 to 1929 and as Warden of New College and a Fellow of Winchester College from 1958 to the present time.

My financial indebtedness to William of Wykeham is therefore great. But there is more to it than that. Anyone with any visual sense who has lived as long as I have in the surroundings created by Wykeham cannot fail to become conscious of the high quality of those surroundings. One becomes aware of the presence and enduring influence of a man who liked the best of everything and had the resources to see that he got it. Even as a schoolboy living in his Winchester buildings I found my curiosity aroused to the point of trying to find out all about them, and this led to an interest in architectural history which has persisted.

This book is an attempt to pay off a small part of my debt by describing and illustrating the buildings and other objects for whose creation Wykeham was responsible. It is not based on any kind of original research, for which I have neither the qualifications nor the inclination; it is derived entirely from secondary sources, rather arbitrarily selected, and is intended less as a contribution to knowledge than as an appreciation of the works of art that owe their existence to the taste, energy and munificence of a remarkable patron.

CHAPTER 1

Wykeham's Life and Character

William of Wykeham has been credited in his time with
the invention of the Perpendicular style of architecture and
of the Public School system. If he had really been the author
of either or both of these peculiarly English institutions he
would have a lot, both good and bad, to answer for.* No
one now, perhaps, believes him responsible for inventing
either of them, though he presumably owes his statue on the
façade of the Victoria and Albert Museum to his supposed
abilities as an architect, and the importance of his contribution to educational development in this country is still
accepted; for instance Oxford's latest historian, Mr Felix
Markham, has written that 'William of Wykeham created
the prototype of the post-Reformation college, which was
undergraduate as well as graduate. The tutorial system by
which the seniors took responsibility for the teaching as well
as the discipline of the juniors was the logical consequence of
the composition of the college.' And there is no doubt that
certain germs of the Public School system, especially its pre-
fectorial elements, can be found in his statutes for Winchester
College.

What is in any case indubitable is that he was one of the
greatest art patrons that this country has ever known. Under
his impulse and at his expense three great architectural com-

* Cf. for instance Gumbril, in Aldous Huxley's *Antic Hay*, reflecting in Eton
College chapel that 'Perpendicular at its best—and its best is its largest—is the
finest sort of English Gothic. At its worst and smallest, as in most of the colleges
in Oxford, it is mean, petty, and, but for a certain picturesqueness, almost
wholly disgusting.'

plexes were created, New College at Oxford, Winchester College and the nave of Winchester Cathedral, which were not only among the major works of their period but are still all in use for the purposes for which he instituted them. Though mauled by succeeding generations they still retain enough traces of their original furnishings for us to see that these too were of the highest quality, and those of Wykeham's own personal possessions that have survived are of the same calibre.

His educational innovations and his political career, both of which were of major importance, are not the concern of this book. But his life, which includes them, must be briefly described as the background against which we can consider the works of art which we owe to him.

He was a self-made man. He was born in 1324 at Wickham in Hampshire, in a family of peasants. Under the patronage of local gentry he received some education in Winchester, presumably at the grammar school attached to the Cathedral. He obtained employment at the royal castle in Winchester, and attracted the attention of William of Edington, then Bishop of Winchester and King's Treasurer, who employed him on his affairs in 1350, the first year he is mentioned in records. By 1356 he was in the royal service, in which year he became clerk of the works at Windsor Castle. It was in this capacity that he first came in contact with the man who was to play a great part in his later artistic activities. This was William Wynford, the mason in charge of the King's works at Windsor. Wynford was, in effect, one of the leading architects of his day, and he was the man whom Wykeham subsequently employed on all his major projects. Moreover the most important building which Wynford was designing and Wykeham supervising at Windsor, the royal lodgings in the upper ward, was one of great interest for the future of Wykeham's works. One of its main features was a hall and chapel placed end to end as part of a single unit (in the nineteenth century they were thrown together to form the present St. George's Hall); this is in turn the main element in the design of both New College and Winchester College, and one which set a pattern followed by almost all mediaeval colleges subsequently built in Oxford.

There is no doubt that Wykeham's work at Windsor established him in his career. There is a not well authenticated legend that he inscribed somewhere on the castle's walls the words 'hoc fecit Wykeham', and when accused of arrogance explained that what he really meant was that 'this made Wykeham'. Certainly the contemporary chronicler John Malverne so interpreted it; 'looking how to please the King and gain his goodwill,' he writes, 'he procured the building of the said Windsor Castle in such a style as one sees it now. . . . On which account, the Lord King enriched him with many good and fat benefices, and soon after made him keeper of his Privy Seal.' And it was of about this period that Froissart wrote 'At this time there reigned a priest in England called Sir William de Wican, and this Sir William de Wican was so much in favour with the King, that by him everything was done, and without him they did nothing.'

In fact, Wykeham soon became too valuable to Edward III to be employed on supervising buildings. In 1363 he became Lord Privy Seal and the King's factotum. He had meanwhile accumulated a large number of ecclesiastical benefices, and in 1366, at the age of 42, he became Bishop of Winchester and thus one of the richest men in England.

The Church was at this time the main avenue to power and wealth open to the ambitious and unprivileged, and of all the positions in the church in England the See of Winchester was one of the richest and most powerful. William of Edington, Wykeham's predecessor as Bishop of Winchester, declined translation to Canterbury on the grounds that 'though Canterbury was the higher rack, Winchester was the deeper manger'. It is indeed notable that the tombs of the mediaeval Bishops of Winchester are far larger and grander than those of the Archbishops in Canterbury Cathedral, and from this period onwards three Oxford Colleges (New College, Magdalen and Corpus) were founded by successive Bishops of Winchester out of their surplus revenues. The enormous diocese extended from the Channel Islands to Southwark, covering the most prosperous area of England, and its revenues have been calculated as being the equivalent of £100,000 a year in modern money (untaxed of course); this may be an under-estimate, and Wykeham could in addition count on the revenue from feudal dues and the income of vacant benefices, as well as the sums he derived from the other benefices he held in plurality. Being celibate, he had no family to support and endow. In the words of Dr Joan Evans, 'there was nothing that such a man could not do'.

What he did at first, however, was in a different field. As soon as he was confirmed as Bishop (after a difficult argument with the Pope) the King made him his Chancellor, that is the head of his government. In this position he was not, perhaps, a conspicuous success, and he resigned it three years later, in 1371. He seems to have been involved in a rather obscure quarrel with John of Gaunt, and in 1373 he was impeached and disgraced. However in 1377, shortly before the accession of Richard II, he was pardoned and had his revenues restored, and he then resumed the work he had already begun before his disgrace, the foundation of New College at Oxford, of which the school at Winchester, though founded later, was from the start intended to be an integral part. New College was building from 1379 to 1386, and again from about 1398 to 1402, and Winchester College from 1387 to 1394. In the latter year the rebuilding of Winchester Cathedral nave was begun. Wykeham was briefly Chancellor again from 1389 to

1391, but his previous taste of politics seems not to have suited him and he withdrew from them again as soon as he could. He died in 1404, in his eightieth year.

What kind of man was he? The inhabitants of the Middle Ages are fairly impenetrable to modern eyes, and successive generations of Wykehamists have constructed their own patterns of their Founder. There are two near contemporary biographies, hagiographical in tone and conveying no real impression of his personality. Bishop Lowth in the eighteenth century saw him as a pillar of the Enlightenment. His Victorian biographers, such as G. H. Moberly, described him as a virtuous anti-Papist, a forerunner of the best type of Anglican bishop. In our own day it is easy for us to visualise him as the ambitious businessman who, having made his pile and having failed in politics, turns to the patronage of education and the arts.

He was of course none of these, or not entirely. We get nearest to him perhaps in the autograph letter owned by New College and reproduced in facsimile as the frontispiece of Moberly's book. Wykeham is writing in haste to Lord Cobham, from the royal palace at Sheen, about some business concerning the Pope and a bill of exchange; the letter is in French, in an elegant, orderly hand, and makes a modern impression in spite of its archaic language; it is just the kind of note that a present-day prime minister might scribble off to a colleague about a bit of important business which he preferred not to handle by telephone. One has the feeling of a capable man of affairs dealing in a matter of fact way with affairs of state on the highest level, involving the King, the Pope and all the powers in the land.

This practical, efficient, modern-seeming side of Wykeham appears too in his educational policy. In his statutes for New College he states as his aim the desire to cure 'the general disease of the clerical army, which we have observed to be grievously wounded owing to the fewness of the clergy, arising from pestilences, wars and other miseries of the world'. But in desiring to refill these depleted ranks he is thinking not only of the Church. He notes the decline in numbers at Oxford, which had formerly produced 'men of great learning, fruitful to the Church of God and to the King and the realm'. To the King and the realm; this is where his main service had lain, and this is the service which the secular clergy, the main intended product and beneficiaries of his foundations, then almost monopolised. They were the civil servants. He was a great civil servant and servant of the State, and his foundations were not only to perpetuate his memory but also to reinforce the service where he had served (a task which, in a different form, they are after a centuries-long interval now at last performing again).

There is another aspect of Wykeham's foundations which may, perhaps, contain a clue to his character. This is their sensible proportion of resources to ends. They were planned in an orderly sequence and completed in all their parts within his lifetime or, in the case of the Cathedral, with resources provided in his will. There is a contrast here with some of his successors. King's College at Cambridge, Eton College, Cardinal College at Oxford were all left as incomplete fragments at their founders' deaths. This was due in part, no doubt, to the political vicissitudes which were more severe in Henry VI's and Cardinal Wolsey's case than in Wyekham's, difficult as the latter's own times were. But they were perhaps also due to the excessive scale on which the later foundations were conceived. Wykeham's ideas, though large, were achievable, and were in fact achieved in his own time. But the cloisters and bell-tower of King's, the nave of Eton College chapel, the cloisters, chapel and second quadrangle of Wolsey's Cardinal College were none of them built, and the buildings that were started either re-

19

I. HEAD OF WYKEHAM, EAST FRONT OF WINCHESTER COLLEGE CHAPEL

2(A) NEW COLLEGE AND THE CITY WALL

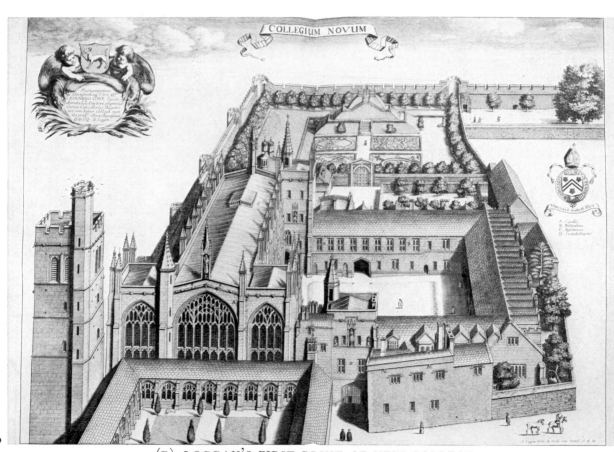

(B) LOGGAN'S FIRST PRINT OF NEW COLLEGE

3(A) NEW COLLEGE, FRONT QUADRANGLE, LOOKING WEST

(B) NEW COLLEGE, FRONT QUADRANGLE, LOOKING EAST

4 NEW COLLEGE, THE ANTE-CHAPEL

5 NEW COLLEGE CHAPEL

6(A) ALL SOULS CHAPEL

(B) NEW COLLEGE BEER CELLAR

7 NEW COLLEGE HALL

8(A) NEW COLLEGE MUNIMENT ROOM, THE VAULT

(B) NEW COLLEGE, THE FOUNDER'S LIBRARY

mained unfinished or had to be completed by subsequent ages. Only when later founders followed Wykeham's pattern closely, if on a slightly reduced scale, like Waynflete at Magdalen or Chichele at All Souls, did they achieve comparably complete results in their own lifetime. Wykeham's efficiency seems to some extent to justify the boastful doggerel attached to his portrait in New College Hall, which has in each corner a picture of New College and of Winchester College:

> 'Qui condis dextra, condis collegia laeva;
> nemo tuarum unam vicit utraque manu.'

('You founded colleges with your right hand and your left; no one with both hands has beaten one hand of yours').

The same good proportion of means to ends seems to prevail in the buildings themselves. They are functionally designed, and continue after nearly six centuries to perform the functions for which they were designed. They are conceived as a whole, and the whole works.

This all seems to add up to the picture of a moderate, efficient, clear-headed executive, competently planning and carrying out well-thought-out designs. But of course the picture has another side. Wykeham lived, after all, in the fourteenth and not in the twentieth century. He was very up-to-date in his century, employing all its best and most fashionable architects, craftsmen and styles, but it was his century and not ours. Almost the only incident in his life as known to us that strikes any kind of personal note is the account of him, as a boy in Winchester, kneeling every morning before an image of the Virgin that stood against a pillar half-way down the nave of the cathedral on the south side, listening to a mass said by one Richard Pekis. Many decades later, as part of his rebuilding of the cathedral, he founded his chantry chapel on this same spot and was in due course buried there. His devotion to the Virgin is apparent in all

w.w.—c

his buildings, in his statutes and in his personal possessions such as his crozier and his jewel. It is not enough to see him as a hard-headed, ambitious politician and businessman, though he may have been that; his religious emotions were very real to him, and very much of his period.

So were his aesthetic reactions, though these are harder to document. But there is one passage in his New College statutes where his feelings become evident. This is where he describes the chapel, 'the image of the most Holy and undivided Trinity, the Holy Cross with the image of the Crucified, the images of the Blessed Virgin Mary and many other Saints, the sculptures, the windows filled with glass, the divers paintings, and many other comely works of art, all curiously wrought and ornamented throughout with various colours, to the praise, glory and honour of God, and of the Virgin Mother'. This seems like personal language. And one would have been inclined to say that it was the language of a man affected by a visual experience, if it were not for the fact that there is no evidence that Wykeham ever visited New College, and some presumption that he never did; his very detailed Register, recording all his movements while Bishop of Winchester, makes no mention of a visit to Oxford, though Cumnor, just across the river, was in his diocese, and the not less detailed Hall Books of New College contain no reference to a visit by the Founder. But at least the passage quoted from his Statutes reflects his interest and pride in the creation of works of art in a religious context.

We do not really know what he looked like. All that the earlier lives tell us in this respect is that he was tall. Portraiture in the modern sense hardly existed in his time, but the statue on his tomb in Winchester Cathedral (frontispiece) seems to be intended as a likeness. At any rate, it is an acceptable image of him, careful, determined, self-confident. The sculptured head of a bishop at the side of the east window of Winchester College chapel (Pl. 1) may well also be a contemporary portrait; that on the other side is an evident likeness of Richard II, Wykeham's patron and, owing to the immense privileges he granted to the College, sometimes regarded as its part-founder.

Before we leave Wykeham's life and come to his works, we ought perhaps to discuss the question of the extent to which he was responsible for them. The old idea that bishops, abbots and monks were the real architects, for whom the masons worked only as builders, has long been abandoned. But the impenetrability of the Middle Ages to our eyes is nowhere deeper than in the obscurity about the status and functions of the mason, the *lathomus*. Was he an architect? Or was he a stone-cutter? No doubt he was really both, and the architect evolved professionally from the stone-cutter. In a sermon preached as early as 1261* we find a denunciation of 'Master Masons with a rod and gloves in their hands, who say to others "cut it for me this way" and labour not themselves yet take higher pay', or again 'in those great buildings there is commonly one chief master who only commands by word of mouth, who seldom or never lays his hand to the job, and yet takes higher pay than the rest'. The great fourteenth-century architect Henry Yevele is described as 'deviser of masonry' to the King.† What seems to emerge from these and similar passages is that the word mason covers everyone from the master mason who was, in the modern sense, the architect of the building, or at least of its stone components, down to the men who actually cut the stones to designs drawn out by the master mason. The restriction to the stone components is important; the carpenters in their sphere were not less important than the masons in theirs, and they were more important in some buildings,

* Quoted in John Harvey, *English Mediaeval Architects*.
† John Harvey, *Henry Yevele*.

for instance at Westminster Hall where the controlling element in the design is the wooden roof designed by Hugh Herland, who also designed for Wykeham the splendid wooden vault of Winchester College chapel.

What then was the rôle of Wykeham, in the royal buildings with which his name is associated and in his own buildings? In the east window of Winchester College chapel (which is a careful nineteenth-century copy of the fourteenth-century glass) there is represented a little group of men (Fig. 1) who are identified as *carpentarius* (almost certainly Hugh Herland), William Wynford *lathomus* (the master mason, the architect of the building apart from its wooden roof) and Simon Membury, the clerk of the works (the glazier, Thomas of Oxford, appears elsewhere in the window).

FIG. 1   Portraits of Herland, Wynford and Membury in the East Window of Winchester College Chapel

The clerk of the works was the man responsible for the supply of materials and labour, for the financial side of the work, and for seeing that the client's requirements were carried out. This was the rôle which Wykeham performed for the King at Windsor and elsewhere, and which Simon Membury later performed for Wykeham at Winchester. It was not a creative rôle. Mr John Harvey deliberately excludes from his great dictionary of English Mediaeval Architects 'such clerical "architects" as Gundulf, Alan of Walsingham and William of Wykeham' on the grounds that 'there is no foundation whatever for the ascription of architectural design in general to monks or clerks in Orders'. In *The King's Works* R. A. Brown and H. M. Colvin write 'however competent the King's clerks may have been as administrators, there is no evidence that any of them (Wykeham included) had any technical knowledge of architecture'.

We can accept all this, and yet not deny to Wykeham his share in the works created under his impulse. Obviously his earlier works for the King had given him an insight into the practice of architecture. Indeed this seems to have been his contemporary reputation; it is generally thought that the contemptuous reference, in a tract attributed to Wiclif, to the clerk who gets preferment because he is 'wise in building castles, or worldly doing, though he cannot well read his psalter' refers to Wykeham, then Chancellor. Wykeham's household accounts show frequent visits to his various palaces by the leading architects of the time: he had been associated with them professionally in the King's works and himself employed them on his own works, and his own concept of his educational and religious requirements must have influenced their designs. This was an age in which architects and other artists were regarded by their patrons and by the public generally as craftsmen, to whom very detailed instructions could be given; contemporary documents giving such instructions exist for painters and sculptors, in which every detail of the composition is laid down by the patron, and no doubt the master masons, the architects, received similar orders. For the architecture of his colleges and his cathedral, as well as for all his other commissions, Wykeham was undoubtedly the patron, not the designer; but he must have been a well-informed and well-qualified patron, able by virtue of his power and wealth but also of his past experience as clerk of the King's works to ensure that he got just what he wanted.

CHAPTER 2

Architecture

A. INTRODUCTORY. WILLIAM WYNFORD

Wykeham embarked on his major architectural works at an auspicious moment. The Perpendicular style, the most characteristically English of all styles of architecture, was just evolving from its tentative beginnings at Wells, Gloucester, St. Stephen's Westminster and St. Paul's cloister, and was receiving its full development in the King's works under the direction of the two great royal masons of the period, Henry Yevele and William Wynford, with whom the not less great carpenter Hugh Herland is generally bracketed. All these men were closely associated with Wykeham and worked for him. Their style was big, strong and bare. The later Perpendicular designers believed that every inch of wall space should be worked over and panelled in intricately geometrical patterns of stone, corresponding to the intricately geometrical window tracery. But these early designers liked great spaces of plain wall, contrasted with massive buttresses, ornamented niches, or windows with strong and not over-elaborate mouldings and relatively simple window-tracery. They developed fully the Perpendicular characteristic of mullions running up vertically from the bottom of the window, through the tracery, to the enclosing arch, but the windows are not the great walls of glass that later became popular. They normally used the depressed four-centred arch only for low entrances; main windows and arcades usually have the higher and nobler two-centred arches.

The whole style is masculine, powerful and restrained.

Of these architects, the one most closely associated with Wykeham is William Wynford (Fig. 1). Not much is known of his life. He is first heard of working at Windsor in 1360, when he is already described as 'Master' and was therefore presumably already at the top of his profession. From then on his association with Wykeham is continuous. When Wykeham became Provost of Wells in 1363 Wynford soon after appeared there as Master Mason, and he probably designed the south-west tower of Wells Cathedral at that time. Later came work for Wykeham at New College (probably) and at Winchester College. In 1394 he was supervising work on Wykeham's manor house at Highclere (of which no trace remains), and in the same year work began under his direction on the rebuilding of the nave of Winchester Cathedral. His son was one of the earliest scholars admitted to New College (as was Herland's). He died in 1405.

Of course Wynford did not work only for Wykeham. He continued to work on royal buildings outside London, including Corfe and Winchester Castles and at Southampton. He seems to have designed a long-since vanished hall for Queen's College, Oxford, and the existing outer gate of Abingdon Abbey was built by him. But the major extant works associated with him are those he carried out for Wykeham. He was one of the greatest architects of his time, indeed one of the greatest of all English architects, and it is really he and not Wykeham who should have his statue among the architects on the front of the Victoria and Albert Museum.

B. NEW COLLEGE, OXFORD

New College was the first of Wykeham's major projects. He had it in mind as early as 1373, but the first band of

I METHUSELAH, NOAH, ABRAHAM (NORTH-WEST WINDOW OF NEW
COLLEGE ANTE-CHAPEL)

2 JUDAH, MOSES, NAHUM (NORTH-EAST WINDOW OF NEW COLLEGE
ANTE-CHAPEL)

3 JESSE WINDOW AT WINCHESTER COLLEGE

(C)

4(A) WYKEHAM'S CROZIER

(B) WYKEHAM'S MITRE

(C) WYKEHAM'S JEWEL

(A)

(B)

scholars whom he assembled then were dispersed at his disgrace in that year and 'went away weeping'. They returned with his return to favour, and by 1379 he had completed his purchase of the site. In the same year the Charter of Foundation was issued, the college being entitled 'Saint Mary College of Winchester in Oxford'. But this title is never used except in official documents, and the College has been called New College practically ever since its foundation. Wykeham's admirers like to think that this was because of the extreme novelty of its plan and scale, though a more prosaic explanation is that there was a pre-existing Oxford college dedicated to St. Mary (Oriel).

The first phase of the building work was over by 1386, when the Warden and Fellows took possession; this consisted of the buildings round the Front Quadrangle. The cloisters were consecrated as a cemetery in 1400 and the bell tower was built at the same time; the barn was being built in 1402.

Whether this collection of buildings, so rapidly erected, really earned the college its sobriquet or not, it was certainly novel. Nothing like it had ever gone up in Oxford or Cambridge before. Little significant college building, indeed, survives at any of the pre-Wykeham foundations at either University, apart from some fine buildings at Merton College, Oxford; and impressive and beautiful as the latter are they do not form part of any unified scheme. But at New College, for the first time at either University, there appears a college complete in all its appurtenances, designed as a whole and built all at one go. Not only this, but it was on a much larger scale than had hitherto been attempted anywhere. Merton, the first Oxford college to be founded and endowed in a substantial manner, provided for twenty-five Fellows. Wykeham's foundation had seventy. New College equalled in numbers and exceeded in endowment all the pre-existing colleges at Oxford added together, and if the twin foundation at Winchester be added to this the scale of his benefaction, and the kind of stupefaction it must have caused, can be appreciated. Of course it has been exceeded by subsequent foundations, and two even of the previously founded colleges, by better management or better luck, are now richer than New College. But at the time it must have seemed a very successful 'Great Leap Forward', and it set a wholly new scale and standard for college foundations. The buildings were in proportion. The Fellows, it is true, lived three or four to a room. But the Warden was housed in some style, and the public buildings are all on a magnificent scale.

These buildings have suffered from the hand of time, and from the varying taste or requirements of successive Wardens and Fellows. But they remain an impressive whole. They are designed in the early Perpendicular style generally associated with Yevele and Wynford. Both of these, as well as Hugh Herland the carpenter, are recorded in the New College hall books and bursars' rolls as having visited the college while structural works were still in progress. Yevele may have given Wykeham some advice; in about 1370 he had designed a quadrangular college at Cobham in Kent, for Lord Cobham, and in 1371 the quadrangular Charter-house in London, both of which may have given Wykeham ideas for his college. But on every ground it seems reasonable to attribute the main design of New College to Wynford. He was certainly responsible for the design of Winchester College, and the two buildings are too alike for it to be reasonable to attribute them to different architects. More-over the previously quoted resemblance to the royal apart-ments at Windsor, also by Wynford, tells in his favour.

The site acquired by Wykeham for his Oxford college lies within the north-east angle of the city walls. One condition of the grant of the land to him was that these walls should be maintained by the college, and they are now in fact the only section of the city's defences that remains intact. The area within them was an insalubrious one, described in a contemporary document as 'full of dirt, filth and stinking carcases ... also there was a great concourse of malefactors, murderers, whores and thieves ... a place as 'twere desolate, and not included or by any occupied'. The population of Oxford, like that of the whole country, had dwindled during the Black Death in 1349 and the following years, and the walls were too large for the city they contained; this had at least the advantage of providing Wykeham with a spacious and well protected site.

The building that Wynford first erected on this fine if derelict site was more than worthy of it (see plan, Fig. 2). It consisted essentially of a well-organised quadrangle, with the chapel and hall on the north side, against the city wall; the muniment tower in the north-east corner; the library on the east side, with the bursary below; chambers for Fellows from the south-east corner along the south side to the south-west corner; and on the west side the main entrance, with a gate-tower in and around which were the Warden's lodgings. To the east projected the kitchen and the long-room (lavatory) and beyond them lay a garden in the angle of the city wall. This collection of buildings set the pattern for the future. No previous Oxford college had begun its life equipped with them all, but in future all new foundations would start with them or strive to acquire them as soon as possible, down to our own times when the chapel, to Wykeham the most important feature of all, tends to be omitted.

At New College all these original buildings still exist, some of them in an altered form, and all except the library are in use for the purposes for which Wykeham commissioned them and Wynford designed them. But the external appearance of the quadrangle suffered severely when in the late seven-

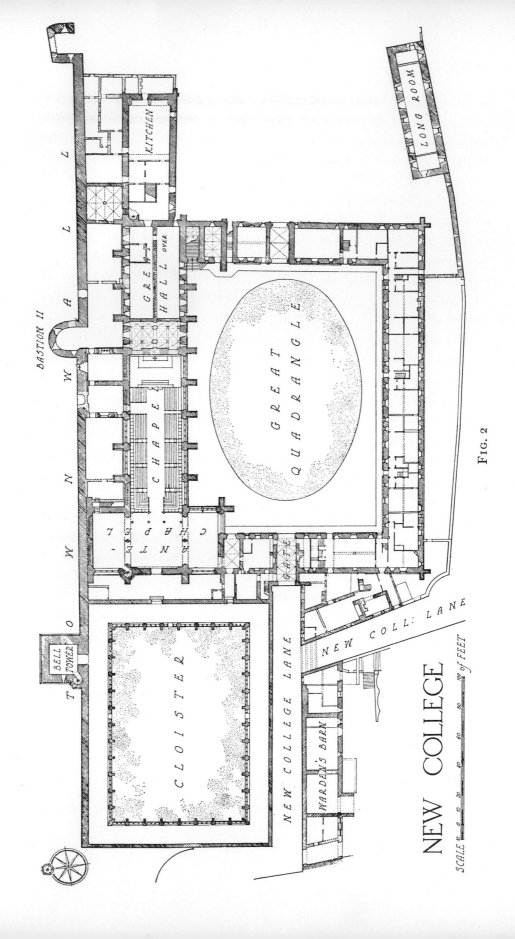

BASTION II

KITCHEN

GREAT HALL OVER

CHAPEL

GREAT QUADRANGLE

ANTE-CHAPEL

GATE

BELL TOWER

CLOISTER

LONG ROOM

NEW COLLEGE LANE

NEW COLL: LANE

WARDEN'S BARN

NEW COLLEGE

SCALE 0 10 20 40 60 80 100 of FEET

FIG. 2

teenth century an extra storey was added to the domestic ranges. Previously these ranges had been of two storeys only, with a sloping roof of stone tiles, as the Chamber Court at Winchester still is and as can be seen in Loggan's first print of New College (Pl. 2B). The domestic ranges were then in proper subordination to the public buildings on the north side, and the gate-tower could be seen as a tower and not merely as a rather pointless protuberance above the roof line. Moreover the windows of the Fellows' chambers were arranged in the façade of these ranges in an interesting and carefully designed grouping round the doorways, and this pattern was destroyed by the addition of the extra storey.

Further damage was done when in the eighteenth century the tracery was removed from all the windows in the domestic ranges. There was really no excuse for this. The extra storey added in the previous century, disfiguring as it is, at least provided much needed accommodation. But the eighteenth-century replacement of Wynford's tracery by sash windows must have been merely a question of preference, an odd commentary on the supposedly impeccable taste of that century.

Though these ranges now look so blank, they are at least less positively repellent since their recent cleaning. Before that time the two lower stories were black with soot, while the upper storey, which was built in the wretched stone habitually used for seventeenth-century buildings in Oxford and had had to be refaced early in this century, was a greenish-yellow. My predecessor, Warden Smith, who particularly disliked the hard dividing line between the two colours, was once seen on a ladder with a bucket of soot and water trying to soften it. The cleaning of the stonework a few years ago has at least reduced both areas to the same agreeable honey colour, though the material is still very diverse.

Whatever one's reservations about the domestic ranges, it remains true that the north range of the chapel and hall can be regarded as perhaps the finest Gothic composition in Oxford. The differing sizes of the chapel and hall windows indicate their differing purposes, but unity is given to the range by the impressive pinnacled buttresses, and balancing though dissimilar high blocks at each end, the ante-chapel to the west and the muniment tower to the east, bind the composition together. Whether seen from the quadrangle from the south or, from the north, rising above the city wall (Pl. 2A), this great range of buildings has a cathedral-like grandeur and a masculine solidity not always achieved in later essays in the same vein.

Impressive as this design is, it is not without flaws. The most notable is the placing of the gate-tower. It is too close to the ante-chapel to make much effect, and the visitor entering by it hardly sees the chapel at all. It would have been much better placed in the middle of the south ranges, which even before its alterations must have been rather blank and could have done with this interruption, while entry from this angle would have given a much more impressive view of the chapel and hall range, as can be seen at Winchester where this mistake has been corrected.

Another odd feature, immediately noticeable as you enter the front quadrangle, is the awkward relationship of the library windows to the arch beneath them. No doubt the position of both is dictated by functional requirements, but only a very small adjustment would have put the point of the arch either immediately below the middle of a window or immediately below a division between two windows, instead of, as at present, below one side of the central window. This is a good case of what Warden Smith, in his history of New College, calls 'a certain untidiness, which often characterises mediaeval building'.

Of all the component parts of the Front Quadrangle the most important is of course the chapel. This is a highly original building. Nothing quite like it had been built before. It is T-shaped in plan, the upright being the chapel proper, which is unaisled and has five bays, while the crosspiece is the ante-chapel, of two bays, with aisles the same height as the nave. There is no real precedent for this plan. It is sometimes suggested that Merton College chapel, which in part antedates New College chapel, is really the first of these T-shaped chapels. But the T-shape at Merton is accidental; it is simply the choir and transepts of a conventional cruciform church, the nave of which was never built though the west front shows clearly that one was intended. No nave was ever planned for New College, and the ante-chapel is not a crossing and does not look like one; Wykeham himself always described it as the nave. This T-shaped plan set the pattern for Oxford college chapels for several centuries. None was ever again built quite on the scale of New College. The most notable are at Magdalen, All Souls and Wadham, and the latest of them, the last dying flicker of the Gothic, was built at Brasenose in 1656. The original purpose of the plan was that the main services would be held in the chapel; the ante-chapel, though it contained four altars, was to be used for 'disputations' and even for college meetings. It was perhaps to enable the Warden to keep an eye on these disputations that there was provided in his private oratory in the lodgings a little double-slit window which commands a view of the ante-chapel.

Quite apart from its originality and its influence on later design, the ante-chapel (Pl. 4) is in itself one of the finest of early Perpendicular interiors. Its most notable feature is the very high and slender pillars and arches that divide the centre from the aisles; the tall and well-proportioned windows are, with one exception, still filled with stained glass of the

Founder's period; there is abundance of plain walling, and the mouldings are massive, firm and restrained.

About the chapel, in its present state, one cannot be so happy (Pl. 5). It has suffered severely. Virtually none of its visible fittings are original. The stained glass is of the eighteenth century, apart from a few fragments of the original glass in the tracery and the canopies. The reredos is a Victorian reconstruction; something similar existed originally but it was destroyed at the Reformation and the east wall was plastered over; when the plaster was removed in the nineteenth century traces of the original work were found, and the present reredos is based to some extent on these. The woodwork, rather too hot in tone, was mostly designed by Sir Gilbert Scott, and though it incorporates a fine series of misericords, 62 in number, and a few other fragments of the original wooden fittings, it makes a busy and overcrowded impression, partly because it has had to be expanded inwards to accommodate a far larger society than Wykeham ever envisaged.

Scott also re-designed the roof. It is not at all certain what the original roof was like. The first illustrations we have of the chapel show it with the plaster vaulting inserted by Wyatt in the late eighteenth century, resembling the one which still covers Magdalen College chapel, and there is no direct record of what this replaced. But I am much obliged to Mr Harvey for having called my attention to a passage in the anonymous *History and Antiquities of Winchester* (actually by the Reverend Richard Wavell) published in 1773, which in describing Winchester College chapel says 'the roof is covered with a ceiling of wood, in imitation of arched stonework, without which, the height would be much too great, as is the case at New College chapel in Oxford, where such a ceiling was in all probability intended; at least, the present rafter-work of that noble chapel, is by no means equal to the

9(A) NEW COLLEGE, KITCHEN ROOF

(B) NEW COLLEGE, LONG-ROOM ROOF

10 NEW COLLEGE CLOISTERS

11 NEW COLLEGE CLOISTERS AND BELL-TOWER

12 NEW COLLEGE LANE

13 WINCHESTER COLLEGE FROM THE TOWER OF WINCHESTER CATHEDRAL

14 WINCHESTER COLLEGE, CHAMBER COURT, LOOKING SOUTH-WEST

15 WINCHESTER COLLEGE, MIDDLE GATE, WINCHESTER CATHEDRAL BEHIND

16 WINCHESTER COLLEGE CHAPEL

magnificence of the rest'. Without adopting Wavell's speculations about the intended vaulting one can, I think, deduce from this that New College chapel was originally roofed as All Souls chapel, which is so closely modelled on it, still is (Pl. 6A), by an open timber roof of the hammer-beam type. If, as seems probable, this was designed by Hugh Herland, it cannot have been one of his more distinguished works. It would have rested, as the roof still does, on the fine row of corbels with alternating heads of Kings and Bishops. The present timber roof, designed by Scott with Herland's roof of Westminster Hall clearly in mind (Scott thought the Westminster roof was 'probably carried out under Wykeham's direction') is not unimpressive internally. But by raising the pitch he has produced an awkward external effect; correspondence in the possession of the college, incidentally, shows that the decision in favour of a roof of this kind was taken by the Warden and Fellows against Scott's recommendations.

With all these alterations it is no longer possible to visualise very clearly the chapel as it was in Wykeham's time. One must imagine the windows with glass like that in the ante-chapel; the reredos less clumsy than now (a former chaplain of the college once likened it in its present state to an unlit gas-fire) and brilliantly painted; an open timber-roof of lower pitch; one line only of stalls at ground level, with wide open floor space and with the woodwork above the stalls not interfering, as the present panelling does, with the sill line of the windows; much colouring throughout, as Wykeham describes it in his statutes, but also much plain walling, as now; and the ten great windows, with their tall silhouettes and handsome tracery, that almost alone remain of the original structure. One would not then, probably, have had the feeling of anti-climax that one now does on entering the chapel from the ante-chapel.

w.w.—D

The hall (Pl. 7) has suffered less than the chapel from the ravages of restorers, though it too contains little more of its original elements than its stone shell. Externally it is the same height as the chapel, but its internal height is less since it is raised up above a ground floor; its interior still appears immensely lofty. It is approached by a steep flight of stairs in the north-east corner of the quadrangle; these stairs are roofed with a particularly elegant piece of lierne vaulting. The hall itself is strikingly mediaeval in feeling. H. A. L. Fisher, the historian, who was Warden of New College from 1924 to 1940, used to maintain that it was the oldest dining-hall in the world with a record of continuous use. Its strongly mediaeval appearance is in part misleading. The excellent linen-fold panelling was, according to tradition, paid for by Archbishop Warham in the early sixteenth century; though mainly Gothic in style it already shows traces of Renaissance influence. The heraldic stained glass (quite good) is Victorian, and so is the open timber roof. The hall was ceiled at the level of the roof corbels in the sixteenth century. It was suspected that the original roof might exist above this ceiling, but when the latter was removed not much was found, and the present roof is largely Gilbert Scott's idea of what might have been expected. All these alterations and insertions, however, leave the general impression of the hall much as it must have been when it was first built, though Warham's panelling is perhaps a good deal more elaborate than anything Wynford or Herland would have inserted.

The hall, itself roofed in wood, is embedded in a complex of stone-vaulted rooms. To the north, between it and the city wall, is the beer-cellar (Pl. 6B), with a splendid ribbed vault rising from a central pillar, like a small, rough chapter-house. To the south is the muniment tower (Pl. 3B), which has on its west face one of the groups of three statues in niches (the Virgin in the centre, the Angel of the Annunciation on the left and Wykeham kneeling in adoration on the right) that occur so frequently in Wykeham's buildings; there are two more at New College, on each side of the Front Gate, and one on each side of the Middle Gate at Winchester. The interior of the Muniment Tower contains four super-posed vaulted rooms, the two lower ones narrow since half the space is occupied by the hall stairs, and the two upper taking the full width of the tower. The upper three of these fine but, alas, largely inaccessible rooms still contain the college archives; a recent recension of them has shown that the rooms are admirably designed for the conservation of archives, being dry, well-ventilated and fireproof. They all have interesting and in some ways unusually designed vault-ing (Pl. 8A) and retain their original tiled floors. The lowest room, with a door opening into the Front Quadrangle, is the college treasury. It contains the college's remarkable col-lection of plate, most of it dating from about 1500, and also a number of Wykeham's personal possessions such as his mitre, his jewel and his rings.

To the south of the muniment tower, on the first floor, is the Founder's library (Pl. 8B). This has been the object of innumerable modifications. I remember it, when I was an undergraduate, as a long, dull room with rather featureless eighteenth-century furnishings. Even with the extra storey above, which contains a library designed by James Wyatt, it soon thereafter became too small for the college's needs, and a new library was built north of the city wall just before the outbreak of the Second World War. The appearance of dry-rot necessitated the removal of all the furnishings from the old library, and it was then found that under the plaster-work there were considerable surviving traces of the original building. It was a long, narrow room of nine bays, with windows whose external appearance clearly marked it off from the rest of the domestic ranges; it comprises a continuous row of large windows, whereas in the Fellows' chambers small and large windows alternate, and the tracery was more elaborate, with a transom, than any others in these ranges with the exception of the two windows of the Warden's hall over the main gate. The library windows can be seen in their original form in Loggan's print (Pl. 2B), and some of them were discovered intact on the east side where they had been walled up when additional buildings were constructed there. A proposal to replace them on the west side caused much controversy in the college at the time of Warden A. H. Smith (1940–1958) and a trial window inserted in the north-west window to show the effect remains in position. But the college eventually decided to retain the sash windows. Inside there were book-cases, with chained books, projecting between the windows, which have window seats. All the original library fittings have of course long since disappeared, and since the room was no longer needed as a library it has now become part of the Senior Common Room. But it has been restored as nearly as possible to its original appearance (though the roof is now flat, owing to the existence of the added upper storey, instead of being an open timber one); its austere double procession of window arches makes it a fine room.

The Fellows' chambers which occupied the south corners and side of the quadrangle have been altered beyond recognition. Originally the Fellows slept either three or four to a room, with small partitioned-off studies in the corners private to each Fellow; the disposition of the windows still reflects these arrangements, though internally all is now entirely different; the large windows lit the common chambers, the small ones the partitioned studies. The windows were always, as now, rectangular on the outside, but had, and in some cases still have, arched openings on the inner side of their thick walls. The larger windows had mullions and cusped heads but no transoms; these would have slightly relieved the present severity of the south range, which now with its sash windows looks very blank.

Most of the west side of the quadrangle is occupied by the Warden's lodgings. The principal rooms in this were and are on the first floor. Over the main gate is the Warden's hall, now known as the Tower Room. The Warden must have dined in some state in this room. As originally designed it had six windows; two looked east into the quadrangle, while the west end of the gate-tower projected beyond the west wall of the college so that the hall had at this end windows looking north and south (these have now been covered up by subsequent buildings but their tracery remains behind the hall's sixteenth-century panelling), as well as two looking west; this was presumably the high-table end of the hall. The Warden was supposed to behave like the abbot of a monastery, keeping his own establishment and only dining in the college hall on rare and festive occasions; a relic of this survives in the custom that when the Warden does dine in hall he does so as a guest and does not normally preside.

In addition to his hall the Warden had a study to the north of it, with a fine oriel window looking into the quadrangle which the eighteenth century pointlessly replaced by two sash windows. Beyond the study was a small oratory adjoining and overlooking the ante-chapel, and in the upper storey of the gate-tower there was a large and many-windowed bedroom, approached by a winding stair which continued up to the top of the tower. The lower stretch of this winding stair was removed when Frogley's grand staircase was inserted in 1675, but the upper stretch to the roof remains. The Warden's accommodation was completed by an enormous kitchen outside the quadrangle to the west.

All these rooms still form part of the lodgings (though the house was much expanded when, at the Reformation, the

Wardens escaped from the obligation of celibacy), and anyone who inhabits them must be conscious, here as elsewhere in the college, of the functional nature of its design. The Founder clearly wished the Warden to keep a sharp eye on everything that went on in the college, and so from his hall, his study and his bedroom he commanded views of the quadrangle, from his oratory he could see into the antechapel, and from his hall and bedroom he could observe anyone approaching the Front Gate, then the only entrance to the college. It sometimes seems to me that the Founder slightly confused the functions of the Warden and the porter, and indeed the present porter's lodge was once part of the lodgings. In any case the placing of the Warden in this position is another of the New College innovations that was widely followed elsewhere. It became standard practice, in college buildings put up after this date in Oxford, to give the Head of the House quarters over the main gate. It is interesting to note that there is an apparently unconscious imitation of this in the situation given to the head of the recently founded Massey College at Toronto University; he, too, in this wholly modern building, lives over the main gate and the porter's lodge.

There are certainly advantages in this position, which are still enjoyed by a present-day occupant of the lodgings at New College, as he sits in the study where his predecessors have sat for nearly six hundred years and looks out onto the Front Quadrangle; undergraduates when told of this are apt to remark 'Ah, I see, Big Brother is watching you.'

On the other side of the college, to the east, there are two projecting arms, the kitchen to the north, adjoining the hall, and the lavatory to the south. Both were presumably situated outside the quadrangle for sanitary and olfactory reasons. The kitchen is a great, high room with an open timbered roof (Pl. 9A), like the hall of a fair-sized college. The lavatory, always known as the long-room, a long, narrow two-storeyed building, originally had closets above and a cess-pit below. It too has a fine open-timbered roof (Pl. 9B), and like so much else at New College must be one of the oldest of its kind in continuous use. It now has bathrooms above and lavatories below, but there is a plan to turn the upper floor into a gallery for the use of the Junior Common Room.

Beyond these two rooms there was and is a large L-shaped garden, bounded on the north and east by the city wall. Access to it is through a double-bayed vaulted passage under the library opposite to, and resembling, the arched main entrance under the gate-tower (all these simple low-pitched vaults in the college, such as these two and the one at the entrance to the chapel and cloisters, are of excellent plain design).

This completes the tally of the buildings put up in the first phase, which ended apparently in 1386. Wykeham and Wynford then seem to have turned their attention to Winchester College, perhaps partly because the land for the further extensions of New College was not yet available. Work started again at Oxford at the end of the century, and was probably complete by the time of the Founder's death in 1404. This second phase included the cloister, the bell-tower and the barn. The cloister (Pl. 10) has very much the air of an after-thought; it lies up against the west front of the ante-chapel but in no particular relation to it; it masks its lower section entirely and the openings are not centred on those of the earlier building, nor is the awkward passage between the two of them anything but an untidy gap. Moreover the cloister itself seems somewhat casually designed; its longer sides have twelve bays and its shorter eight so that the openings (the west walk has none) cannot be centrally placed. With all this it is a place of great charm; its tracery, as always at New College, is well designed in a sober way, and inside the walks the timber arches of the roof, like the ribs of an inverted ship, lead the eye agreeably along. The cloister is the college burial ground, but it was also used for study and discussion in the summer. I once took an American visitor in there on a warm day in Trinity Term and observed a Fellow of the college conducting a philosophy class on the lawn in the centre; this seemed to my visitor, and rightly, to be the essence of traditional Oxford.

North of the cloister rises the bell-tower (Pl. 11), which is built as a bastion of the city wall and so projects beyond it. It is not, it must be admitted, among the more distinguished of Oxford's towers, being merely a kind of plain stone structure, almost unadorned, designed to push bells up to the requisite height in the air. This is of course how modern architects, if they have to, design bell-towers. But one would not judge from his towers built for Wykeham that Wynford was much of a hand at tower-building. His tower at Winchester College was taken down within less than a hundred years of its being built, and his New College tower has never been much admired. Yet Mr Harvey tells us that 'his was probably the greatest single influence which made the church towers of Somerset the finest in the country' and his tower at Wells Cathedral is a satisfactory complement to the early thirteenth-century west front. Perhaps Wykeham himself was not interested in towers. His Cathedral at Winchester lacks them, apart from the squat Norman tower at the crossing.

The last of the Founder's buildings at New College to be completed was the barn. This lies south of the cloister, and besides being used for the storage of provender from the college farms probably contained guest-rooms, as is suggested by the traceried window in its east end, one of the few of Wynford's domestic windows at New College to retain intact its tracery and even its shutters.

17 WINCHESTER COLLEGE HALL

18(A) WINCHESTER COLLEGE, OLD SCHOOL-ROOM (SEVENTH CHAMBER)

(B) WINCHESTER COLLEGE
BEER CELLAR

19 WINCHESTER COLLEGE FROM THE WARDEN'S GARDEN

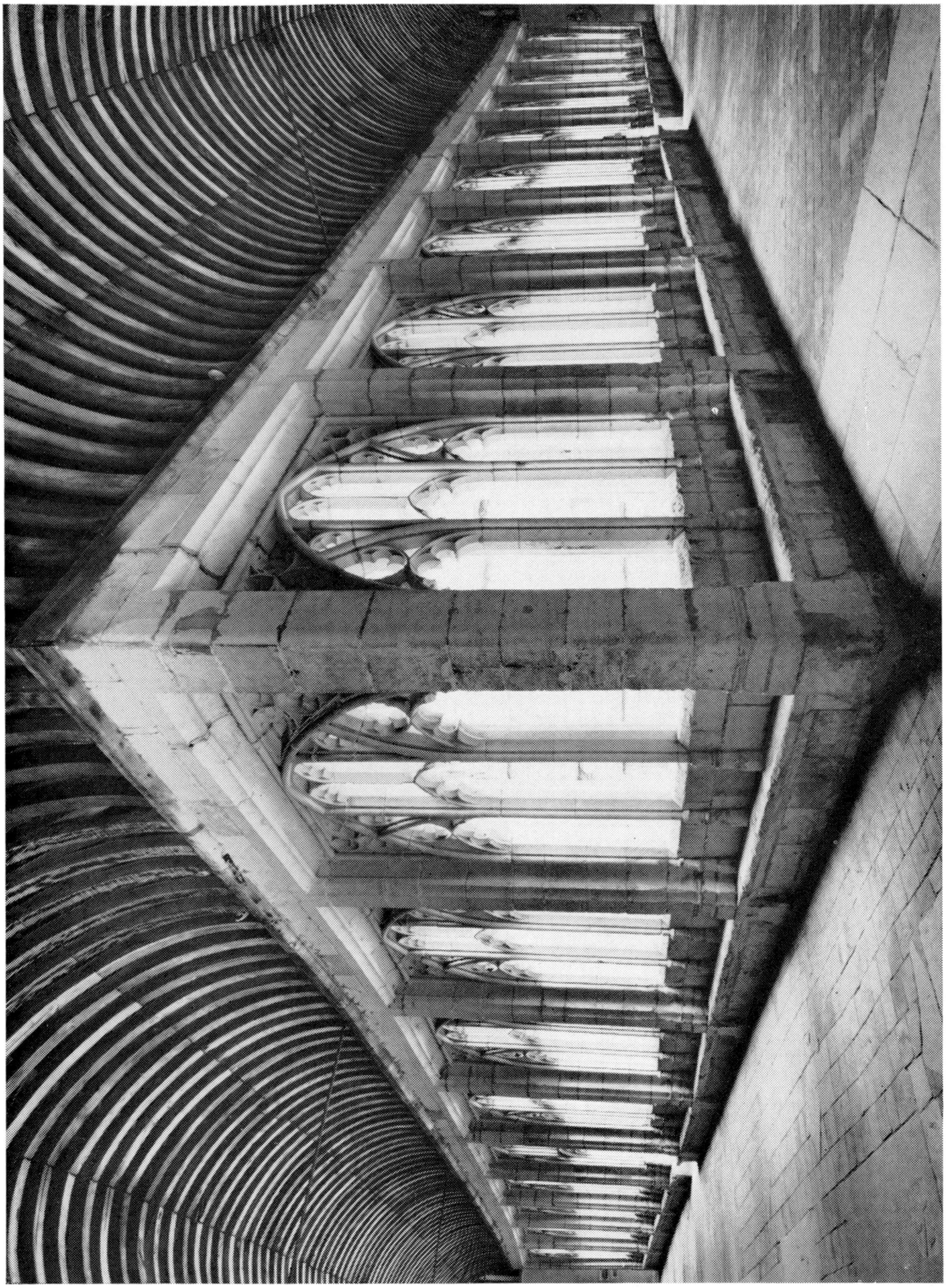

20 WINCHESTER COLLEGE CLOISTERS

21 WINCHESTER CATHEDRAL NAVE, NORTH SIDE

22 WINCHESTER CATHEDRAL NAVE, INTERIOR FROM THE WEST

23 WINCHESTER CATHEDRAL NAVE, INTERIOR LOOKING SOUTH-WEST

24 WINCHESTER CATHEDRAL, WYKEHAM'S CHANTRY

The blank north wall of the barn and the blank south wall of the cloister flank the narrow lane (Pl. 12) that leads to the Front Gate, 'that grim ravine', as Max Beerbohm described it in *Zuleika Dobson*, 'by which you approach New College'. Indeed New College is virtually invisible from the outside. Perhaps for reasons of defence, necessary in the troubled time of its foundation, it turns blank and forbidding walls to the exterior, over which occasional glimpses of pinnacles and turrets give some hints of the glories within. Only from the north, in the days of its foundation, could a traveller approaching across the fields have seen a splendid line of buildings rising high above the city wall and the moat, and now even this view has disappeared behind the four towering storeys of Gilbert Scott's New Buildings on Holywell. But once inside the forbidding outer walls there is still plenty to be seen.

C. WINCHESTER COLLEGE

As soon as the first stage of New College was completed, Wykeham and Wynford turned their attention to Winchester College. Wykeham had started as early as 1373 to maintain a 'grammarian' and scholars in his cathedral city, and in 1382 he sealed at Southwark the Foundation Deed of the future college at Winchester. Work started in 1387, the year after the Warden and Fellows of New College took possession of their buildings, and the Warden and Fellows of Winchester were able to enter theirs in 1394. The site was an agreeable one, in the water-meadows just south of the Cathedral and the Bishop's Palace of Wolvesey, outside the city walls, between fast-flowing trout streams.

The buildings put up in these attractive surroundings bear a strong family resemblance to those of New College, on a slightly reduced scale. When I was an undergraduate at New College I had hanging in my rooms the Loggan print of

Winchester, and many of my non-Wykehamist friends, looking at it casually, thought it represented the Front Quadrangle of New College. But the general impression made by the Winchester buildings is lighter and perhaps more elegant than those of New College. The material is better. Now that New College has been cleaned its surface is no longer actively unattractive, as it used to be, but it does not have much positive charm. On the other hand the Binstead stone from the Isle of Wight, of which the chapel and hall at Winchester are built, is one of the most beautiful of all English building materials, and is well matched by the silvery flint-work of the domestic ranges. And Winchester College has suffered less, at least externally, from the ravages of its Warden and Fellows than New College has from those of its Warden and Fellows. No extra storey has been added to Chamber Court, which retains its proper proportions and is, in fact, one of the most satisfactory quadrangles in England. It requires much less effort of the imagination to visualise Wykeham's Winchester College than Wykeham's New College.

It is possible also to conceive that Winchester College, being built later than New College, may incorporate certain improvements that suggested themselves to Wykeham or to Wynford as the work at Oxford proceeded (see plan, Fig. 3). The better position of the gate-tower has already been noted (above, page 48). Winchester has two courts or quadrangles to New College's one, and the second at Winchester, Outer Court, contains a number of offices not provided at New College such as a slaughter-house and a bakery; possibly these were necessary because Winchester College, being unlike New College outside the city walls, had to be more self-contained. But certainly the entry to Winchester, through the lower Outer Gate, Outer Court (almost double its present length before the Warden's new lodgings usurped its

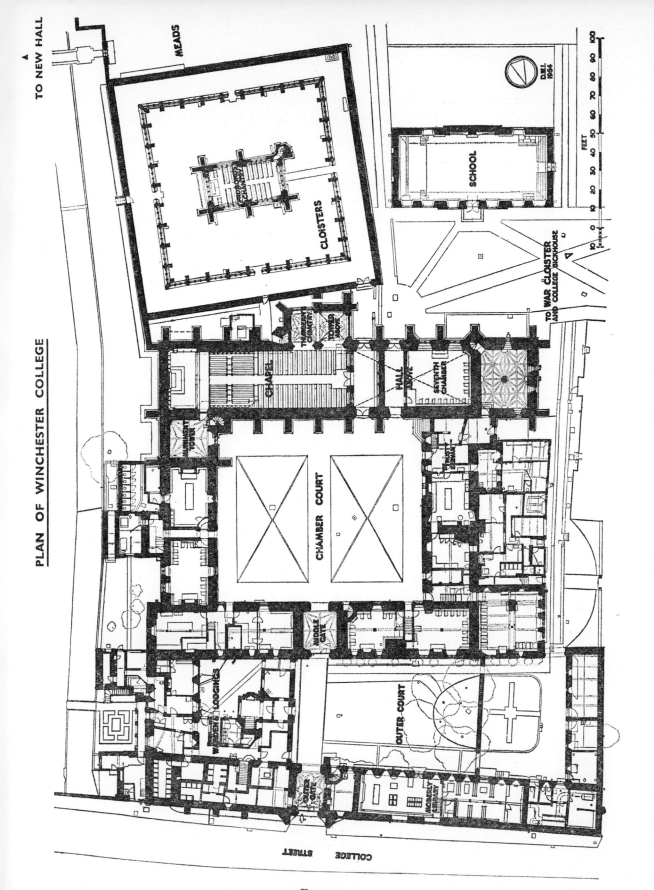

PLAN OF WINCHESTER COLLEGE

TO NEW HALL

MEADS

CLOISTERS

CHAPEL

THURBERN'S CHANTRY

TOWER ABOVE

HALL ABOVE

SEVENTH CHAMBER

FROMOND'S CHANTRY

CHAMBER COURT

MIDDLE GATE

WARDEN'S LODGINGS

OUTER COURT

TOWER GATE

MOBERLY LIBRARY

COLLEGE STREET

SCHOOL

TO WAR CLOISTER AND COLLEGE SICKHOUSE

D.W.I. 1954

FEET

FIG. 3

eastern half) and the high Middle Gate that brings you in directly facing chapel and hall, is much more impressive than the sidelong manner by which you enter the Front Quadrangle at New College.

Winchester College, like New College, and for the same defensive reasons, presents a rather forbidding exterior to the street. Its north front, by which alone the public originally had access, consisted at first only of the low blank wall, topped by a sloping stone-tiled roof, of the brewery, slaughter-house, bakery and other domestic buildings that formed the north side of the Outer Court, almost window-less and pierced in the centre only by the two-storey Outer Gate. This somewhat fortress-like exterior was modified, even originally, by the beautiful statue of the Virgin and Child in a niche over the gate (Pl. 27), and has now been further softened by the agreeable eighteenth-century brickwork of the new Warden's lodgings that rises up on top of the old wall to the east.

As you enter through Outer Gate you are faced by Middle Gate. This has the usual group of three statues (the Virgin flanked by Gabriel and Wykeham) on each face. In it, as at New College, the Warden had his quarters, a hall over the gate and a bedroom above, but unlike the Warden of New College he abandoned his original rooms when the Reformation abolished clerical celibacy and he needed larger accommodation for his family, which he secured by building up the eastern half of Outer Court. Chamber Court, which is entered through Middle Gate, is the heart of Winchester College (Pl. 14 & 15). The chapel and hall are on its south side, and so their position is reversed by comparison with New College, with the chapel to the east of the hall; but as at New College they form one great range, with the hall raised up above a ground floor and reached by a stair in the corner of the court, as at New College. The buttresses in this range are less imposing than those at New College and have no pinnacles. The muniment tower is in the south-east corner, against the chapel. The school-room was under the hall, and the kitchen is not, as at New College, outside the main complex but occupies most of the west side of the court (perhaps some better method of controlling cooking smells had by then been discovered). The ground-floor rooms in the other ranges were chambers for the scholars, and the first floor was occupied by the Fellows, the chaplains and the two masters. There seems to have been no room specifically provided as a library (the old brewery in Outer Court was converted for this purpose in quite recent years); probably boys were thought to have less need of books than Oxford students. There is a conduit, over a well which still produces remarkably sweet, cool water, under a low arch in the western wall. The mediaeval lavatory, which no longer exists, was outside the east range of Chamber Court, abutting on the branch of the Itchen that flows by it; this no doubt accounts for the name used for this stream in the School, Logie, a good old-fashioned English word for excrement.

As at New College most of these rooms are still in use for the purpose for which they were built. The Fellows have disappeared (the present Fellows are no more than non-resident Governors), but the seventy scholars of the Foundation still work in the chambers (which now include the old school-room), worship in the chapel, and eat food in the hall, prepared in the kitchen, that Wykeham provided and Wynford designed; they have usurped the Fellows' rooms as dormitories. The buildings are not, perhaps, entirely convenient as a modern boarding-school; communal living is dictated by them, no one has a private study, and exposure to the weather is considerable. But the compensations are great. The sense of continuity is one of them, but the greatest is the continual crossing and recrossing of that beautiful courtyard, changing constantly in all lights and weathers but most enchanting, perhaps, on summer evenings with swifts faintly screaming as they circle round and liquid light filtering down over the brown and cream stone and grey flints.

The most important of the buildings on Chamber Court is of course the chapel, as at New College, and as at New College it is the building which has suffered most, internally, from restoration. It is entered from a passage under the east end of the hall. This passage is now much disfigured by the school's Crimean War Memorial; from it a door leads left into the chapel, between two double-light traceried windows. The first sight of the interior of the chapel (Pl. 16) can be something of a shock. The collegiate arrangement of inward-facing stalls has been replaced by tightly packed rows of eastward-facing pews, in light oak carved in a pallid Edwardian Gothic style; the panelling is in the same manner, and the stained glass has the hard, bright virulence of the early nineteenth century. But, looking again, the bones of a good building are seen still to be there. As at New College, there are fine, tall windows with handsome tracery, well set in good plain walling. Wynford's big, bare style is still evident. And the roof, unlike that of New College, is a masterpiece. Herland's oak roof of Westminster Hall has been described as 'the greatest single work of art of the whole of the European Middle Ages', and the roof of Winchester College Chapel is the second greatest work of this very great master. It is totally different from his Westminster roof, being in a form approximating to fan vaulting, very light and elegant in design. As I remember it as a boy it was dim brown and gold, like a rich old bookbinding, but during recent repair work it came to light that it had been originally painted white, to resemble stone-work, with details picked out in colour, as the similar wooden vaulting in the choir of Winchester Cathedral has always been, and it has been restored to this condition.

Winchester College chapel has no structural ante-chapel comparable with that at New College. Instead, the two western bays were divided off from the four to the east by a rood screen (the door which gave access to it can still be seen in the south wall). This division was retained when the chapel was repanelled in the late seventeenth century, but it was swept away in the Victorian refitting necessitated by the much increased size of the school, and the interior of the chapel is now all one undivided space; the side chapel opening to the south off the two westernmost bays is an addition of the late fifteenth century. Apart from eighteen misericords, none of the original fittings of the chapel remain *in situ*. It has to depend for its effect on its fine proportions and its noble roof, and these luckily remain unchanged.

The hall (Pl. 17), to the west, is very like a reduced version of New College hall, though its plain Tudor panelling produces a much less sumptuous effect than that created by Warham's linenfold at Oxford. It too has none of its original fittings left; the open timber roof dates only from 1819, but it is very much in Herland's style and must replace and reproduce one designed by him. The good modern glass by R. M. Y. Gleadowe makes the room far less dark than its Oxford equivalent, and it gives one a feeling of bare, airy height.

The main range of buildings continues for one long bay to the west of the hall. This bay contains various service rooms; on the ground floor there is a fine vaulted beer cellar (Pl. 18B), with a central pillar, which reversing the usual order of things is considerably larger, higher and handsomer than that at New College; did schoolboys then drink more beer than undergraduates?

The muniment tower, at the other end of Chamber Court, is very like the one at New College but with only three storeys instead of four, and with only the two lower rooms vaulted. It composes very well with the east end of the chapel when seen from the Warden's garden across Logie (Pl. 19).

The ground-floor rooms round Chamber Court, the chambers where the scholars live and work, give a perhaps misleading impression of having remained unaltered since the foundation (the rooms on the first floor, on the contrary, have obviously all changed beyond recognition). One of the ground-floor chambers, Seventh (Pl. 18A), has altered more than most; it is part of the original school-room (part has become a passage-way). A. F. Leach describes it as 'the oldest school building in England', and one can perhaps accept this while admitting that no one has actually been taught in it since Warden Nicholas employed Wren or one of his assistants to design the new School opposite. An enthusiastic school poet, writing in about 1647, dilates in Latin on the amenities of this old school-room: 'in winter the sun warms us with his whole lamp, and as there is no fire-place we warm ourselves in Phoebus's rays and the breath of his mouth', while in summer the breeze blows cool from the trees in Meads. A hardy race.

Immediately to the south of the chapel was the bell-tower. This tower is something of a mystery. It no longer exists, having been taken down when Warden Thurbern in the late fifteenth century built his chantry chapel to the south of the chapel, with the present chapel tower over it. The only evidence for the appearance of the original tower is a drawing of Winchester College in a manuscript of about 1460 by Warden Chandler of New College. This shows the tower, astonishingly, as round, and capped with a spire. A round tower at that date and place would have been unique and is scarcely probable. But Chandler's drawing of Winchester is so inaccurate in all its other details (as compared with the drawing of New College in the same manuscript, which has

(B) BROUGHTON CASTLE, THE GATEWAY

25(A) SOUTHWARK CATHEDRAL

83

26(A) CARVING FROM THE
REREDOS OF NEW COLLEG
CHAPEL. THE ANNUNCIATI

(B) CARVING FROM THE
REREDOS OF NEW COLLEGE
CHAPEL. THE NATIVITY

some correspondence with actuality) as to suggest that it was based on a sketchy recollection.

South of the tower lies the cloister (Pl. 20), which here as at New College was something of an after-thought and looks it, though its relationship to the chapel is less awkward than at Oxford. Indeed the whole design is better, though the scale is slightly smaller; it is a square of nine bays a side, so the entrances to the garth can be in the centres of the sides, and there is agreeable stone panelling inside the walks which is missing at Oxford. Winchester College cloister's most unusual and indeed unique feature is post-Wykeham; this is the two-storeyed chantry chapel built in its centre by Wykeham's steward, John Fromond, who died in 1420. It adds to the charm of this delightful place, whose past use for summer study survives in Winchester's name for the summer term, Cloister Time.

All this group of buildings looks splendid from Meads, the field to the south, which is surrounded by an ancient wall and planted with huge planes. It would look better still if it were not partially masked by the seventeenth-century School which, handsome as it is from the front and inside, turns a rather bald brick back on Meads. But seen from almost any side except the entrance in College Street, Winchester College presents a more gracious and less forbidding aspect than New College. It is less grand but more appealing.

D. WINCHESTER CATHEDRAL

As soon as he had got his two academic communities installed in their new buildings, Wykeham turned his attention to his cathedral.

Winchester Cathedral, the longest mediaeval cathedral in Europe, owes its present shape principally to the Norman Conquest. Winchester was one of William the Conqueror's

w.w.—g

capitals, and its Saxon cathedral was demolished to make way for one of the most enormous of the many enormous churches that were being put up all over the country from about 1070 onwards. When Wykeham became Bishop most of this Norman work remained. A magnificent Early English retro-choir had been built, mainly to house the shrine of St. Swithun, and the remodelling of the choir had begun. But the transepts and the nave retained their original Norman form, except that under Wykeham's predecessor, Bishop Edington, the Norman west front had been replaced by a new one in a rather undistinguished, even parochial-looking, early Perpendicular style and the two westernmost bays of the north aisle had been remodelled. What the Norman work was like can still be seen in the transepts, or in the very similar nave of Ely Cathedral. The Winchester nave was immensely long, as were those of all these major Anglo-Norman cathedrals. It had fourteen bays (the two westernmost bays were suppressed during Bishop Edington's rebuilding). It was plain, even crude, but massive and dignified; the bays were divided into three equal parts, arcade, triforium and clerestory; there was not much ornament, and the stones were small and the mortar-joints thick. It was the kind of thing that is admired more now than it would have been in the fourteenth century. I remember as a boy being shocked by a master at Winchester who described William of Wykeham as a vandal for having destroyed it, but then this particular master had spent most of his early life in the shadow of Ely Cathedral. In the fourteenth century and even earlier, anyone who could afford to replace or rebuild a building of this kind did so; Henry III, for instance, for all his reverence for Edward the Confessor did not hesitate to demolish Edward's Westminster Abbey.

When Wykeham decided to remodel the nave of his

cathedral at his own expense, in about 1394, there is no doubt that he entrusted the work to Wynford, and in his will sealed in 1403, a year before his death, Wykeham provided that the work should continue under Wynford's direction. (Wynford actually died in 1405, only a year after Wykeham.) The presence in the string-course above the main arcade of a number of representations of Richard II's badge of the white hart suggests that the work must have been complete

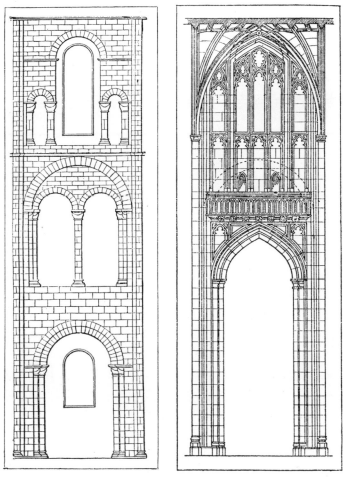

FIG. 4   Winchester Cathedral, showing original design of
nave and reconstruction by William of Wykeham

up to at least this level by the time of that monarch's deposition in 1399. The vaulting bosses contain numerous representations of the royal arms; some of these are in a form abandoned in 1405, which suggests that part at least of this vault, presumably the last part of the work to be undertaken, was finished before that date, while others are in the new form adopted after 1405. Whatever the completion date, it is clear that the work was commissioned and designed under Wykeham's impulse, and that he paid for it, in his lifetime and by legacy. Simon Membury was clerk of the works, as at Winchester College.

The procedure used was a remarkable one (Fig. 4). At Canterbury, shortly before, the Norman nave had been entirely swept away and replaced by a new one, probably designed by Henry Yevele. Wynford was less drastic. The core of the Norman uprights was retained, and in the earliest stage of the work even the small Norman facing-stones were recut and reused, though later on new facing-stones were placed on the retained core. The three Norman divisions were replaced by two, the triforium being suppressed and the space it had occupied being divided between the arcade and the clerestory. Finally a lierne vault in stone replaced the wooden Norman roof.

Externally, this remodelled nave is plain, heavy and massive (Pl. 21). The north aisle has buttresses and pinnacles closely resembling those of New College chapel and hall. The interior (Pl. 22) is a very different matter. James Fergusson, the father of English architectural history, wrote that 'in our own country no building is more entirely satisfactory than the nave at Winchester, where the width of the pillars exceeds that of the aisles, and the whole is Norman in outline, though Gothic in detail', and he thought that Wykeham's transformation of the nave produced 'the most pleasing and satisfactory arrangement adopted during the middle ages'. Mr Harvey, in his biography of Yevele, prefers the latter's nave at Canterbury, but he too has written of the Winchester nave as 'one of the supreme triumphs of English Gothic', and he considers that Yevele at Canterbury and Wynford at Winchester 'share the credit of designing the two finest Perpendicular interiors now existing'. Mr Harvey thinks that Wynford's design at Winchester was limited by the decision to utilise the Norman fabric, which conditioned the main lines of his new arcades; but it is also possible to hold, with Fergusson, that this decision gives the Winchester nave a solidity which the Canterbury nave somehow lacks.

The virtual absence of any good stained glass (apart from a mosaic of fragments in the west window) is noticeable in the nave at Winchester, and it is a pity that it terminates to the east in a rather feeble Victorian screen and the somewhat incongruous Norman arch at the crossing; one misses the solid rood screen that once stood there on the still surviving Norman piers (Pl. 23), and perhaps even more the Inigo Jones screen that replaced it and was removed by the Victorians. In this respect the Canterbury nave is better off. But even as it is the Winchester nave is very impressive, and deserves the praise it has so often received. The main arcade is lofty and well-proportioned, resembling in profile and in much detail the arcade in New College ante-chapel. The clerestory windows are small by Perpendicular standards, the space round them being covered in good plain stone panelling. One of the finest features of this interior, and a point of superiority over Yevele's work at Canterbury, are the massive vaulting shafts that rise uninterruptedly from the bases to the springing of the vault. This is in fact part of the original Norman work, as can be seen in the north transept, and the effect is splendidly columnar, with the vault spreading out at the top like branches from great trunks, while between the columns the horizontal line of bosses and the parapeted passage that replace the triforium lead the eye along from end to end.

In one of the bays on the south side of this great nave, on the spot where, as a child, he had daily heard Pekis's mass, Wykeham founded his chantry chapel and is buried. The chapel (Pl. 24) completely fills the space between two pillars, and reaches up its elaborate openwork screen to the level of the arcaded parapet. It has a delightful miniature vault, below which lies, quite undamaged, the tomb and effigy of the bishop. There appears to be no evidence at all for the agreeable legend of the Wykehamist but Puritan Colonel Fiennes, with sword drawn, defending his Founder's tomb against the iconoclastic fury of his own troops. But however the tomb came to survive, it is the most elegant of all Wynford's work for Wykeham.

E. OTHER BUILDINGS

A new chancel was built for the collegiate church of St. Martin-le-Grand in London at Wykeham's expense in 1385–6, with Yevele as the architect. No trace of this remains.

The Priory Church of St. Mary Overie, now Southwark Cathedral, which had always enjoyed the patronage and support of the Bishops of Winchester, was severely damaged by fire in 1385. The west front was rebuilt, perhaps under Wykeham's influence, in a style suggesting that Yevele was involved. This front has disappeared, but the first stage of the central tower above roof level (Pl. 25A) seems also to be of this period; certainly the window design is almost identical with that of New College hall.

As Bishop of Winchester Wykeham had a number of official residences, the most important being Wolvesey in Winchester, Farnham Castle on the way to London and

Southwark in London. There is no record that he commissioned any important work at any of these, or even at Bishop's Waltham in Hampshire which seems to have become his favourite residence and was the place of his death.

At Highclere, between Winchester and Oxford, he had a manor at which work was done by men whose names are now familiar in these pages, Wynford, Herland and Thomas Glazier. No trace of this remains; the site is entirely covered by the enormous Gothic mansion built by Barry for the Earl of Carnarvon, and its fish-ponds have become artificial lakes.

In 1377 Wykeham bought the manor of Broughton in north Oxfordshire. This he settled on his great-nephew, Thomas Perrott, who became his heir and took the name of Wykeham; the latter's descendants, the Twistleton-Wykeham-Fiennes family, the head of which is Lord Saye and Sele, still live at Broughton. Most of Broughton Castle is either earlier or later than Wykeham's time. But the gatehouse (Pl. 25B) looks as if it dates mainly from the end of the fourteenth century, and is therefore likely to have been built or rebuilt while Wykeham owned the manor; if so it is interesting as the only surviving example of domestic architecture commissioned by him.

CHAPTER 3

Sculpture

The principal architectural works commissioned by Wykeham provided space for considerable sculptural ornament. There were innumerable carved bosses and corbels; the external bosses have mostly perished from the effects of the weather, but there are fine series of corbels surviving in the chapels and halls of New College and Winchester College, and there is a great deal of carved ornament in the nave of Winchester Cathedral; the line of bosses along the string-course above the nave arcade is especially fine.

More significantly, there were niches in which statues or groups of statues were placed. Much the most important of these was the reredos of New College chapel. This covered the whole east wall up to the roof, and probably contained four rows of statues of saints in niches. As already mentioned it was almost completely destroyed at the Reformation; of the sculpture there remained only five fragmentary panels, now preserved in the choir practice-room, whose original site was no doubt the position immediately above the altar now occupied by Sir Richard Westmacott's reliefs. The fourteenth-century reliefs depict respectively the lower half of two seated draped figures (probably the Coronation of the Virgin, or perhaps the Visitation); the Annunciation (Pl. 26A) (fairly complete); the Nativity (Pl. 26B) (with a nice carving of the ox and the ass in wickerwork stalls); what seems to be the Ascension, or conceivably the Baptism of Christ (much damaged); and the lower half of what is clearly the Resurrection. They are all in a style not unlike that of

27 WINCHESTER COLLEGE. STATUE OF THE VIRGIN ON THE OUTER GATE

28 (A & B) MISERICORDS FROM NEW COLLEGE CHAPEL

(C & D) MISERICORDS FROM WINCHESTER COLLEGE CHAPEL

the English alabaster reliefs of the same period, though less crowded than the latter generally are.

Then there are the five groups of three statues, representing the Annunciation with Wykeham himself in adoration, which have already been mentioned; there are three at New College (one each side of the Front Gate and one on the muniment tower) and two at Winchester College (one each side of Middle Gate). These at New College are heavily restored and scarcely recognisable as mediaeval objects; those at Winchester are unrestored but badly perished. Apart from testifying to Wykeham's especial devotion to the Annunciation these groups provide effective ornament to the buildings on which they are placed, without being (so far as their present state enables us to judge) particularly important as works of art in themselves.

The Statue of the Virgin and Child over the north face of Outer Gate at Winchester College (Pl. 27) is a different matter. This too is useful as architectural ornament. But it has gentle, smiling merits of its own, 'one of the loveliest masterpieces of late fourteenth-century English sculpture', as Professor Hawkes has written, rather simpering perhaps for modern tastes but graceful and charming, softening the austerity of Winchester College's grim exterior.

In addition to these there were large and important statues in the gable pinnacles at the east and west end of the chapel and hall ranges at both New College and Winchester, and in the gable pinnacle in the west front of Winchester Cathedral, which was completed by Wynford during Wykeham's episcopate; these have all been replaced by modern statues.

Apart from the statue in the west pinnacle, the only important sculpture in Winchester Cathedral commissioned by Wykeham was that in his chantry chapel. This too had a reredos, but the statues now in its niches are modern. His effigy, however, still lies on the tomb, the head supported by two angels and with three lively figures of monks at his feet (frontispiece). The figure of Wykeham himself is vigorous and life-like; it is hard not to believe that it was carved by someone who knew him in life. This was contemporary practice, witness the effigies of Wykeham's two royal masters, Edward III and Richard II, in Westminster Abbey, and it seems reasonable to suppose that it was followed in Wykeham's case.

None of the sculpture commissioned by Wykeham is of outstanding artistic merit, though it is as good as anything else of its time. What is remarkable is that so much of it survives. The Reformation destroyed most of the visible sculpture in Winchester and Oxford, and it is odd that the 'Mariolatrous' images on Wykeham's colleges were left intact. They had their effect. A generation after the Reformation, so Anthony Wood tells us, one of the many recusant Fellows of New College, afterwards reconverted, ascribed his sojourn with Rome to 'the lively memorials of popery in statues and pictures on the gates and in the chapel of New College'.

Perhaps this is the place to mention the wood-carving commissioned by Wykeham. The only notable survival of this is the magnificent series of misericords in New College chapel, and the much smaller but not less interesting set in Winchester College chapel. These misericords (Pl. 28), which are difficult to see, are an astonishing product of the mediaeval imagination. Portraying swans and peacocks, sirens, gryphons and basilisks, human masks and foliage, elegant architectural details and violent street brawls, their variety is extraordinary and their accomplishment remarkable. Judging by Winchester and New College, carving in wood had more vitality than carving in stone at the end of the English fourteenth century.

CHAPTER 4

Stained Glass

Both at New College and at Winchester College, and quite probably in the nave of Winchester Cathedral, Wykeham employed a glass-painter called Thomas Glazier of Oxford. It is his portrait (Fig. 5) which appears at Jesse's feet in the east window of Winchester College chapel, Wynford, Herland and Simon Membury being grouped at his head.

Thomas Glazier first appears in the New College records as dining in hall there in August 1386. Thereafter, for the next twelve years, he dined regularly in hall four or five times a year, from 1388 onwards dining with the Fellows (this admission to the high table is of some interest for the light it sheds on the social status of craftsmen like Thomas Glazier in the middle ages). He went on working for the college after Wykeham's death, and died between 1421 and 1427. In 1393 it is recorded that the stained glass for Winchester College was transported from Oxford via Highclere to Winchester. There is no record of his having done any work for Winchester Cathedral, but the few fragments that remain in the nave

Fig. 5 Portrait of Thomas Glazier in the East Window of Winchester College Chapel

windows there are in his style. Wykeham left elaborate instructions in his will about the glazing of the cathedral windows, and it is reasonable to suppose that the same glass-painter who had worked for him at his two colleges (and at his house at Highclere) would have been employed again in the cathedral.

The fate of Thomas Glazier's glass at the two colleges was a curious one. In both cases it survived the ravages of the Reformation and the Civil War. But at New College almost all Thomas Glazier's glass in the chapel proper, and quite a quantity of it in the ante-chapel, was removed in the eighteenth century and replaced by contemporary glass, of varying merit. At Winchester the Warden and Fellows, between 1822 and 1828, sent the glass for repair to a Shrewsbury firm, Betton & Evans, who made a careful copy of it which they sent back in place of the original.

Both at New College and at Winchester College most of the windows were originally filled with single figures of saints and patriarchs, under canopies. At New College, however, the two six-light east-facing windows of the ante-chapel had four representations of the Crucifixion, flanked by St. Mary and St. John, in their lower lights, above the four altars, and the east window at Winchester and the central west window at New College contained representations of the tree of Jesse.

Much more of Thomas Glazier's glass remains at New College than at Winchester. The ante-chapel is entirely glazed with it, except for the central west window where the Jesse used to be. Some of the glass is not where it was; the crucifix panels have been replaced by glass removed from the chapel, presumably at the Reformation. But from many angles the ante-chapel seems to be entirely glazed with its original glass, and very effective this is (Colour plates 1 and 2). The backgrounds are silvery, and the tall hieratic figures wear robes of olive-green, purple, rose-pink, umber or pale blue; the monotonous red-white-and-blue effects of so much glass of this date are largely avoided. The tracery lights for the most part contain figures of angels, though in some there are figures of the Wise Virgins, of Wykeham adoring the Trinity and other subjects; some of the tracery lights in the chapel retain their original glass.

This is some of the very best glass surviving anywhere from the fourteenth century, and we have no clear record of why the eighteenth-century Warden and Fellows decided to remove so much of it. Perhaps it was once again an affair of eighteenth-century taste. But perhaps the glass had already begun the process of corrosion and discoloration which has affected some of Thomas Glazier's New College glass and is even more noticeable in the surviving fragments of his Winchester glass. In any case all his glass in New College chapel proper, except for some tracery-lights and one or two small details, disappeared at this time, and so did the major west window of the ante-chapel. New College has now what must be the best series of eighteenth-century windows in England; but it is sad that this should have been gained at the expense of so much first-class mediaeval glass.

The history of the west window is interesting. In 1765 a York glass-painter, William Peckitt, completed a commission to fill the window with new glass. The College did not like Peckitt's new glass when they had got it, and ten years later turned it out and replaced it with Sir Joshua Reynolds's famous window, for long one of the principal sights of Oxford. But Peckitt had already been paid for his window. In his bill there is an item 'I alow for the Old Glass . . . £30'. This 'Old Glass' seems to have been part at least of the original Jesse Window, and Peckitt succeeded in placing this in York Minster, where it can now be seen in the three-light window over the entrance to the Zouche chapel in the south choir-aisle, with some rather startling borders designed by Peckitt himself. In a letter to the Warden about a later transaction of a similar kind Peckitt wrote 'I am very indifferent of purchaceing the Old Glass; for that which I took out of the Great West Window I could not dispose of readily after it was taken down.' He would find no such difficulty now, and a suggestion made after the Second World War by Warden Smith to the then Dean of York that the New College Jesse be returned to its original place was coldly received. It is in fact stained glass of the first quality, which makes its mark even in York Minster, that great treasure-house of mediaeval glass.

The Winchester College glass survived a little longer, and then suffered the fate described earlier in this chapter. The Betton & Evans copy is quite faithful as to drawing, and so reproduces for us in tolerable accuracy the composition and arrangement of Thomas Glazier's glass. But the colours are terrible. Thomas Glazier's soft olive-green has become a harsh emerald, his rose-pink and aubergine have turned to puce and magenta, and the thin, flat glass has no tonal quality. Some of the original glass from the Jesse Window has been reassembled and put in the west window of Thurbern's chantry, and so it is possible to contrast it directly with the 1820 copy; the contrast is painful. The best of these recovered pieces is the upper part of the Virgin and Child that represents the summit of Jesse's tree (Colour plate 3); this and the other figures from the tree are extremely attractive in tone and colour, with their intersecting vines and leafy backgrounds. Three figures from side windows are in the Victoria and Albert Museum, and others are in a private collection in America. The Victoria and Albert figures (Pl. 29) are seen from too close and look coarse in their present position; it is a pity that they cannot be returned to Winchester, where they would look better from the angle from which they were designed to be seen (the Victoria and Albert Museum has already been very generous in placing a figure from the Jesse Tree on loan with the other recovered pieces). On the other hand a small figure of a Wise Virgin, removed from a tracery light in New College chapel and now set in an internal window in the Warden's lodgings there, shows delightful drawing which can never have been visible in its original position (Pl. 30A).

It is possible that the Winchester glass at least, though undoubtedly put together in the workshop of Thomas Glazier at Oxford, was designed by the painter Herebright of Cologne. Herebright was a distinguished artist employed by Wykeham on work at two of his residences, Farnham Castle and Esher Place, in 1393 (he also painted a great altarpiece for Old St. Paul's in 1398), and the style of the Winchester glass would accord with a Rhineland background.

CHAPTER 5

Goldsmiths' Work and Jewellery

Of the original Chapel plate at New College and Winchester, which must certainly have been very lavish, nothing survives. Indeed, nothing of this kind of work remains at Winchester College, apart from the college seal (see below), the so-called 'Founder's Spoon', whose connexion with Wykeham is tenuous, and one plain gold ring with a sapphire. But New College retains a remarkable collection of objects belonging to Wykeham, of which the most important, his crozier, has been since the eighteenth century exhibited in a case let into the north wall of the chapel, while the remainder is in the college treasury.

The crozier (Colour plate 4A) was left to New College by Wykeham in his will. When and where it was made is a matter of some doubt. It has in the past been generally assumed to be of English workmanship. Lethaby, for instance, noted an analogy between the design of the niches and canopies below the crook and that of the Eleanor Crosses, and suggested that a jeweller working on Cheapside may have copied this part of the crozier from Cheap Cross; this has long since vanished, but it presumably was on the pattern of the crosses at Waltham or Northampton (Pl. 30B). More recent writers have suggested a possible Italian origin, and there are interesting resemblances with the crozier from Reichenau on Lake Constance, which is now in the Victoria and Albert Museum; this has very similar crockets round the crook, which is supported by an angel very like that on Wykeham's crook and, like it, is decorated with translucent

29 THREE FIGURES FROM WINCHESTER COLLEGE CHAPEL, NOW IN
THE VICTORIA AND ALBERT MUSEUM

(A)

30 (A) WISE VIRGIN (NEW COLLEGE, FORMERLY IN THE CHAPEL, NOW IN THE WARDEN'S LODGINGS)   (B) ELEANOR CROSS, NORTHAMPTON

enamels, though the whole effect is much less elaborate. The similar and slightly later Limerick crozier bears the name of an Irish craftsman.

The date of Wykeham's crozier is as obscure as its origin. Sir William St. John Hope and other writers have suggested that on stylistic grounds the staff at least must be earlier than 1366, the date of Wykeham's accession to the episcopate, the implication being that it cannot have been made for him (though no one questions that it was in his possession and is the one bequeathed by him to New College in his will; the rather improbable suggestion is that he bought it second-hand, which would be hardly in character). Certainly the architectural details of the upper section show no traces of the Perpendicular style; their resemblance to the Eleanor Crosses of the preceding century has already been noted. But there is no reason to suppose that jewellers necessarily followed the latest architectural fashions; it will be seen from the recto frontispiece that the seal which Wykeham had made for Winchester College in about 1393 has architectural detail which resembles work of more than a century earlier. Of course if the crozier is of continental origin one would not expect Perpendicular detailing. The analogous Reichenau crozier can be exactly dated to 1351.

Whatever its origin or date Wykeham's crozier is certainly a magnificent object. The shaft has elegant silver plates with figures of lilies, and above this there breaks out a splendid profusion of miniature architecture in silver-gilt, with figures of saints in niches backed with enamel. This leads via a nice little battlemented building to the crook, which is supported by an angel with outspread wings and lined with translucent enamels, in brilliant colours, showing angels playing various musical instruments (including a barrel organ, a penny whistle and bagpipes). Within the crook there is a kneeling figure of John the Baptist. He is adoring a little group of the

w.w.—h

Annunciation which is clearly out of place and has in fact only recently beeh placed there; it is not shown in this position in eighteenth-century engravings of the crozier, and St. John Hope suggests that it really belongs on the little battle-mented building lower down. Hope thought that there should have been a figure of the Virgin and Child here, and it will be noted that there is one in this position on the Reiche-nau crozier and another on the Limerick crozier.

Besides the crozier, Wykeham left New College his jewelled mitre (Colour plate 4B). This, much reconstructed, is now in the college treasury. It used to be kept in the Warden's lodgings, where it had collapsed into what St. John Hope has described as 'an apparently hopeless mass of tangled and crumpled gold tissue intermixed with strings of seed pearls', together with four silver-gilt crocketed borders and a number of jewels set in various patterns. Hope's own reconstruction of all this was, it is said, discredited by the action of Sir Hercules Read, a rival antiquarian, who by placing it on his head demonstrated that if Hope was right Wykeham must have been of more than mortal size. A more convincing reconstruction, since made, has the disadvantage of omitting some objects always associated with the mitre, including three uncut emeralds set in gold and a series of enamelled and jewelled tablets set in bands. These tablets show monkeys (some playing musical instruments), stags, hares and dogs; the colour and technique of the enamel closely resembles that on Wykeham's crozier. It is possible that they were attached to the labels which hung down be-hind the mitre. The component parts of this mitre are so sumptuous that, even if we cannot be sure how they were put together, we can be certain that it was originally a glittering and splendid affair.

There is one other object of comparable status associated with Wykeham and possessed by New College, though no record of its transmission to the college exists, and that is what is traditionally called the Founder's Jewel (Colour plate 4c). This is in the form of a Lombardic M (for Mary) about $2\frac{1}{4}$ inches high, of reddish gold set with rubies, emeralds and pearls (some of which are missing). Within the M are beautifully modelled gold figures of the Virgin and the Archangel Gabriel; between them, on the upright, is the pot of lilies usual in representations of the Annunciation; the pot is a ruby and the lilies are in green and white enamel. The figures are stylistically very close to those on Wykeham's crozier. This again is a luxuriously beautiful object.

The case in the treasury which contains the mitre and the jewel also contains three other objects associated with him. The first is the large silver seal which he gave to the college in 1379 (Recto Frontispiece). This, as is usual with any object associated with Wykeham, includes a representation of the Annunciation. He gave a similar but smaller silver seal to Winchester College in about 1393 (Recto Frontispiece). The other two are two rings, one a small, plain gold ring with a single ruby, perhaps the one left to him in his will by his predecessor William of Edington, and the other a massive silver-gilt ceremonial affair, to be worn over a glove, with a big, flawed crystal.

CHAPTER 6

Conclusion

So there it is: three major buildings; some minor sculpture, and some lively woodwork; no surviving paintings; some first-rate stained glass; some resplendent personal possessions. It is a substantial achievement. No doubt Wykeham's main motive was the perpetuation of his name, and in this he has been successful; the term Wykehamist is as widely known now as it has ever been. But another motive must certainly have been the love of beautiful things and the desire to create them, and here again he has been successful. Apart from reigning monarchs, who may be thought to have an unfair advantage, it is difficult to think of another English patron who has had so much influence on the course of English art until we reach Lord Burlington. There are one or two interesting analogies between the two of them. Neither of them was himself an original creative artist, but both had practical experience of architecture, and both by their patronage gave an impulse to a style which they did not invent but which, partly as the result of their patronage, established itself for generations as the leading English style and gave birth to a large number of peculiarly English buildings. Of course Perpendicular Gothic is more peculiarly English than Palladianism, which had its roots in Italy. But in many an English village the Perpendicular parish church stands alongside the Palladian mansion in a combination which only England can show. Burlington's relationship to Kent and Colin Campbell was not unlike Wykeham's to Wynford and Herland. Both sets of architects and patrons were to some extent in a reaction against a more ornate style (Decorated Gothic and the school of Wren, Vanbrugh and Hawksmoor) and preferred a relatively unornamented manner of design depending largely on good proportions and careful detailing.

Wykeham's followers at Oxford were William of Waynflete, Bishop of Winchester and founder of Magdalen College, and Henry Chichele, Archbishop of Canterbury and founder of All Souls College. Both were, so to speak, from Wykeham's stable; Waynflete had been Headmaster of Winchester, and Chichele was educated at Winchester and New College and had been a Fellow of the latter. Their college buildings resemble those of New College but on a diminished scale; at Magdalen Waynflete economically combined the cloister and the quadrangle into one, and at All Souls the quandrangle is so small that there is no room in it for the hall, which had to be placed outside it to the north. The style in both cases is still bare in the Wynford manner, but some of the strength has gone out of it; the buttresses are weaker and the pinnacles spindly. At Magdalen, at least, all is redeemed by the magnificent bell-tower, and at both colleges the governing bodies have done less damage to the original structure than at New College, though at All Souls Chichele's hall and cloister were destroyed when the Hawksmoor quadrangle was built.

However Wykeham's most notable follower was of course Henry VI. He visited Winchester and New College repeatedly, he made presentations to the former and increased the endowments of the latter, and when he founded Eton he took from Winchester not only the Headmaster and some of the scholars but even earth for the foundations and cloth for the scholars' gowns. In his instructions for the design of Eton College chapel the King repeatedly refers to the dimensions of New College chapel as those which he wished emulated, and the nave at Eton, if it had ever been built, would probably have been on the lines of the New College ante-chapel, but prolonged because of its intended double use as a parish church. At King's College, Cambridge, the projected but unexecuted detached cloister, lying to the west of the chapel and with a bell-tower at one side, was as the authors of *The King's Works* say 'undoubtedly derived from New College'. It is perhaps not too fanciful to suggest, too, that Henry was influenced even in regard to the style of his buildings by Wynford's work at New College and Winchester; he laid down that the chapel at King's College was to be 'in large fourme, clene and substanciel, settying a parte super-fluite of too gret curious workes of entaille and besy moldyng'. Wynford's manner could hardly be better described.

The Wars of the Roses prevented the completion of Henry's projects, and when they were over the kind of private patronage that Wykeham, Waynflete and Chichele had exercised did not reappear, except perhaps in Wolsey's abortive foundation of Cardinal College. Rich men built themselves great houses, of course; but the greatest of them were scarcely on the scale of even one of Wykeham's founda-tions, and they lacked the social purpose that has kept Wykeham's colleges alive and prosperous while the great houses decay all around us. Only the state, taking over from the monarchs, can order now the kind of works that Wyke-ham instituted, and it must, alas, be doubted whether the state will ever prove as enlightened a patron as Wykeham was.

Acknowledgments

My debt to Mr. John Harvey will be sufficiently clear from the text. But in addition he has been kind enough to read the book in typescript and to offer me some very useful criticism, advice and help, demolishing in the process several fancy structures of conjecture which I had erected.

I am also indebted for advice and help to Mr. Francis Steer, Mr. Ruthven Hall, Mr. W. J. Carpenter-Turner, Sir Michael Adeane, Mr. Ralph Arnold, Mrs. Edgar Lobel and the late Lord and Lady Saye and Sele.

Finally I am most grateful to my secretary, Mrs. Victoria Banbury, for her skill and patience in decyphering my untidy manuscript.

Note on the Illustrations

The Frontispiece and Plates numbers 1, 13–17, 18A, 19–24, 25A and 28 c and d are from photographs by Mr. Albert W. Kerr. Nos. 13–17, 18A, 19, 20, 27 and Colour Plate No. 3 are the property of Warden and Fellows of Winchester College and are reproduced with their permission.

Plates Nos. 2–12, 25B, 26, 28 A and B and 30A and Colour Plates 1, 2 and 4 are from photographs by Mr. J. W. Thomas. Nos. 2, 4, 5, 7 and 10–12 are the property of the Warden and Fellows of New College and are reproduced with their permission.

Plates Nos. 18B and 30B are from the National Monuments Record.

Plate No. 29 is supplied by the Victoria & Albert Museum and is reproduced with their permission.